ARMORED (THYREOPHORA) DINOSAURS

CLASSIFY THE FEATURES OF PREHISTORIC CREATURES

DINO-SORTED!

SONYA NEWLAND

Gareth Stevens PUBLISHING

Please visit our website, www.garethstevens.com. For a free color catalog of all our high-quality books, call toll free 1-800-542-2595 or fax 1-877-542-2596.

Cataloging-in-Publication Data
Names: Newland, Sonya.
Title: Armored dinosaurs / Sonya Newland.
Description: Buffalo, NY : Gareth Stevens Publishing, 2026. | Series: Dino-sorted! | Includes glossary and index.
Identifiers: ISBN 9781482473544 (pbk.) | ISBN 9781482473551 (library bound) | ISBN 9781482473568 (ebook)
Subjects: LCSH: Ornithischia--Juvenile literature. | Ornithischia--Classification--Juvenile literature.
Classification: LCC QE862.O65 N483 2026 | DDC 567.914--dc23

Published in 2026 by
Gareth Stevens Publishing
2544 Clinton St.
Buffalo, NY 14224

First published in Great Britain in 2020 by
The Watts Publishing Group

Credits
Editor: Sonya Newland
Designer: Clare Nicholas

The publisher would like to thank the following for permission to reproduce their pictures:

Alamy: Dorling Kindersley Ltd 6, Stocktrek Images, Inc. 10t, The Natural History Museum 19b, MasPix 21, Lou-foto 26, Mohamad Haghani 27b; Getty: Roberto Machado Noa 18; Shutterstock: Warpaint cover, 4r, 7b, 8, 9t, 15b, 16–17, 24–25, 28–29, Linda Bucklin 4l, Michael Rosskothen 5t, 11t, 17, 25, Catmando 5b, 20–21, Ralf Juergen Kraft 7t, 27t, Algonga 9bl, Zhenyakot 9br, Danita Delmont 10b, topimages 11b, Ton Bangkeaw 12, Herschel Hoffmeyer 12–13, Daniel Eskridge 13, 19t, 22–23, Martin Weber 14, Pecold 15t, AKKHARAT JARUSILAWONG 23.

All design elements from Shutterstock.

Printed in the United States of America

CPSIA compliance information: Batch #CSGS26: For further information contact Gareth Stevens at 1-800-542-2595.

PRONUNCIATION GUIDE

Allosaurus (AL-oh-SORE-rus)

Ankylosaurus (an-KIE-loh-SORE-us)

Euoplocephalus (you-OH-plo-kef-ah-luss)

Gargoyleosaurus (gahr-goy-lee-oh-SORE-us)

Gigantspinosaurus (JY-gant-spy-no-SORE-us)

Huayangosaurus (hoy-YANG-oh-SORE-us)

Kentrosaurus (KEN-troh-SORE-us)

Miragaia (mi-ra-GAI-uh)

Nodosaurus (no-doh-SORE-us)

Pinacosaurus (pin-ak-oh-SORE-us)

Polacanthus (pol-a-KAN-thus)

Saichania (sigh-chan-EE-a)

Scelidosaurus (skel-EYE-doh-SORE-us)

Scutellosaurus (skoo-tell-oh-SORE-us)

Stegosaurus (steg-oh-SORE-us)

Talarurus (tal-a-ROOR-us)

Tyrannosaurus rex (tie-RAN-oh-SORE-us recks)

Velociraptor (vel-OSS-ee-rap-tor)

CONTENTS

MEET THE

DINOSAURS CAN BE SORTED INTO GROUPS THAT SHARE CERTAIN FEATURES. THYREOPHORA MEANS "SHIELD-BEARER," BECAUSE MEMBERS OF THIS GROUP ALL HAD SOME KIND OF ARMOR. THYREOPHORA BELONG TO A CATEGORY OF DINOSAURS CALLED ORNITHISCHIANS, WHICH MEANS "BIRD-HIPPED."

Gargoyleosaurus

Polacanthus

Armored dinosaurs evolved in the Early Jurassic Period. Small, early thyreophora, such as *Scelidosaurus* and *Scutellosaurus*, were the first to have bony plates, called scutes, on their bodies as a form of protection. Over the millions of years that they existed, thyreophora developed larger, tougher scutes.

EARLY JURASSIC DINOSAURS

Scelidosaurus
Scutellosaurus

MID JURASSIC DINOSAURS

Huayangosaurus

LATE JURASSIC DINOSAURS

Gargoyleosaurus
Kentrosaurus
Miragaia
Stegosaurus

JURASSIC PERIOD

(201 to 145 million years ago)

THYREOPHORA

Gigantspinosaurus

As well as scutes, the thyreophora evolved to have other types of armor, such as spikes on their body or clubs on their tail.

All dinosaurs, including the thyreophora, were wiped out in a mass extinction event 66 million years ago. Scientists believe that a huge asteroid crashed into Earth in the area that is now Mexico, filling the air with deadly gas and dust. This changed the climate so dramatically that few living things could survive. At the end of the Cretaceous Period, three-quarters of life on Earth died out.

LATE CRETACEOUS DINOSAURS

Ankylosaurus
Euoplocephalus
Gigantspinosaurus
Pinacosaurus
Saichania
Talarurus

EARLY CRETACEOUS DINOSAURS

Nodosaurus
Polacanthus

CRETACEOUS PERIOD
(145 to 66 million years ago)

STEGOSAURS AND ANKYLOSAURS

EXPERTS DIVIDE THE THYREOPHORA INTO TWO GROUPS ACCORDING TO THEIR FEATURES. THE STEGOSAURS ARE THE "PLATED DINOSAURS," AND THE ANKYLOSAURS ARE THE "ARMORED DINOSAURS."

Stegosaurs and ankylosaurs evolved from Early Jurassic ancestors. Stegosaurs emerged first, in the Mid Jurassic Period. Some survived into the Cretaceous Period. Many were wiped out in an extinction event at the end of the Jurassic era. Ankylosaurs came later in the Jurassic Period. They lived until the end of the Cretaceous Period.

An early ancestor of the thyreophora, *Scelidosaurus,* may have been able to rear up on its two back legs. It had rows of bony scutes along its back and sides.

Stegosaurs and ankylosaurs all have some form of bony plates as armor, but they also have different features, which is what characterizes the two groups. Stegosaurs had rows of upright bony plates running down their back and tail. They were bigger and had longer legs than the ankylosaurs.

Ankylosaurs were further divided into ankylosaurids and nodosaurids. Ankylosaurids like *Talarurus* had a club at the end of their tail, which the nodosaurids didn't have.

The ankylosaurs had a different body shape to the stegosaurs. Although some ankylosaurs were big, they were lower and broader than their stegosaur relatives. Their armor plates lay flat and covered more of their bodies. Many ankylosaurs also had spikes on the back of their head and body.

Gargoyleosaurus was one of the earliest ankylosaurs, living in the Late Jurassic Period.

SORTED:

QUICK FACTS

PERIOD:
Late Jurassic

LIVED IN:
Europe

LENGTH:
20 feet (6 m)

WEIGHT:
up to 4,410 pounds(2,000 kg)

MIRAGAIA

STANDING AT ABOUT 6.5 FEET (2 M) HIGH, *MIRAGAIA* WAS SMALL FOR A STEGOSAUR. BUT IT HAD SOME FEATURES THAT MADE IT STAND OUT.

PLATES AND SPIKES

A double row of upright triangular plates ran down *Miragaia*'s neck and back. These curved inwards slightly on the inner side. *Miragaia*'s spikes may have been on its shoulders or perhaps on its tail.

LONG NECK AND LEGS

With 17 vertebrae, *Miragaia*'s neck was longer than that of any other known stegosaur. Its front legs were also long. Paleontologists think that *Miragaia* may have evolved with these features so it could feed on taller plants.

ANKLYOSAURUS

ANKYLOSAURUS GAVE ITS NAME TO THE ANKYLOSAUR SUB-GROUP OF THYREOPHORA. THE NAME MEANS "FUSED LIZARD." IT WAS CALLED THIS BECAUSE THE BONES IN ITS BODY AND SKULL WERE OFTEN FUSED TOGETHER.

QUICK FACTS

PERIOD:
Late Cretaceous

LIVED IN:
North America

LENGTH:
33 feet (10 m)

WEIGHT:
up to 15,400 pounds (7,000 kg)

BODY SHAPE

Ankylosaurus was one of the biggest ankylosaurs. It had a very broad body–almost as wide as it was long! It walked on all fours, supporting its weight on its thick legs.

ARMOR

Ankylosaurus was covered from head to tail in armor. It had scutes all over its body. The big spikes on its head may have been strong enough to break the teeth of any carnivore brave enough to try and take a bite. The tail club was made of strong, fused bones.

DINOMIGHTY!

It might look broad and squat, but *Ankylosaurus* was a big animal–twice as long and three-and-a-half times as heavy as a rhinoceros!

VARIED SIZE

THE EARLIEST THYREOPHORA WERE SMALL. SOME LATER SPECIES GREW TO BE A LOT BIGGER AND HEAVIER, BUT THROUGHOUT THEIR TIME ON EARTH THE ARMORED DINOSAURS CAME IN A RANGE OF SIZES.

Scutellosaurus, the earliest known thyreophora, was small and light. It grew up to 4 feet (1.2 m) long and weighed around 20 pounds (10 kg)–about the same as a large turkey! *Scutellosaurus* had a slender tail and small, bony plates on its back. This light body structure meant it could walk on two legs.

▶ *Scutellosaurus* had short arms compared to the size of its back legs, but it may still have moved on all fours some of the time.

▶ Fossil footprints left in rock can give us information about the size of a dinosaur and whether it walked on two legs or four.

Scientists describe body structures like the stegosaurs' as "graviportal." That means they are physically adapted to move slowly over land because they weigh so much. The giant tortoise is an example of a modern graviportal animal.

As the group evolved, some species developed thicker armor that covered more of their strong, heavy bodies. This extra weight meant that they couldn't walk on two legs any more. From about 180 million years ago, all thyreophora were quadrupeds–walking on all fours.

It's difficult to know which were the smallest and largest species of thyreophora. Experts can only guess based on the fossil bones they have found. It's very unusual to find a complete dinosaur skeleton.

Using fossils like this *Ankylosaurus* skull, paleontologists can work out the approximate size of the whole dinosaur.

SORTED:

STEGOSAURUS

STEGOSAURUS WAS PROBABLY THE LARGEST OF ALL THE THYREOPHORA. THESE BIG, SLOW-MOVING, SOLIDLY BUILT DINOSAURS ROAMED NORTH AMERICA IN THE LATE JURASSIC PERIOD.

QUICK FACTS

PERIOD:
Late Jurassic

LIVED IN:
North America

LENGTH:
30 feet (9 m)

WEIGHT:
6,600 pounds (3,000 kg)

SIZE

Stegosaurus grew up to 30 feet (9 m) long and 12 feet (3.7 m) high. Weighing up to 6,600 pounds (3,000 kg), it would have had to eat huge amounts of plant matter to survive. In 2014, a nearly complete *Stegosaurus* skeleton was found in Wyoming. This helped paleontologists understand a lot about this dinosaur, such as how fast it could move.

HEAD AND NECK

Despite its big, wide body, *Stegosaurus* had a small head. Its brain was probably only the same size as a dog's! It also had a short neck. This suggests that *Stegosaurus* kept its head close to the ground, eating low-lying plants and shrubs.

ARMOR

Stegosaurus had two uneven rows of bony upright plates along its back. Some experts think that the plates acted as a cooling system, like how an elephant's big ears channel heat away from its body. Others think the plates were for display–perhaps used to attract a mate. At the end of its tail, *Stegosaurus* had bony spikes, each one up to 35 inches (90 cm long).

DINOMIGHTY!

The plates on a *Stegosaurus*'s back could be up to 24 inches (60 cm) wide by 24 inches (60 cm) high–about the same size as a bicycle wheel!

STURDY LEGS AND FEET

APART FROM THE VERY EARLIEST THYREOPHORA, ALL THE DINOSAURS IN THIS GROUP WERE QUADRUPEDS—THEY WALKED ON FOUR LEGS. PALEONTOLOGISTS THINK THAT SOME OF THEM MAY HAVE BEEN ABLE TO REAR UP ON THEIR HIND LEGS TO REACH HIGHER PLANTS.

The thyreophora all had strong, thick, pillar-like legs to support their heavy bodies. Stegosaurs' back legs were usually more than twice as long as their front legs. Ankylosaurs also had longer back legs, although not as long as the stegosaurs'.

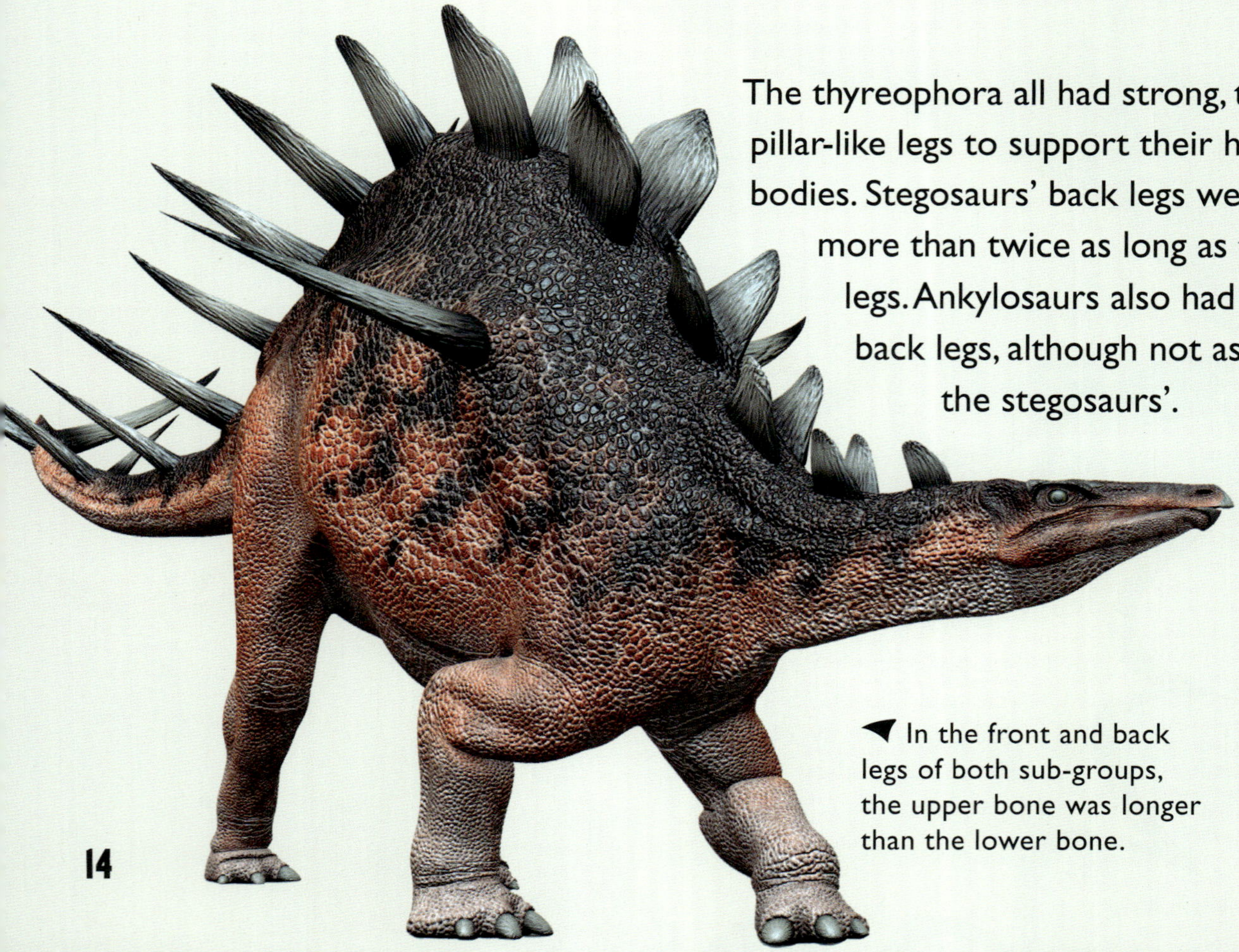

In the front and back legs of both sub-groups, the upper bone was longer than the lower bone.

All the thyreophora had bony feet a bit like hooves. Some stegosaurs, including *Stegosaurus*, had five toes on their front feet and three on the back. Later ankylosaur fossils show three toes on their hind feet. Some kinds may have had five.

The foot bones were short in thyreophora. Combined with their leg structure, this probably made moving around very cumbersome for these dinosaurs. They would have had a short stride, so were not well adapted for running. The short-legged ankylosaurs could probably reach top speeds of only 6.2 miles (10 km) per hour.

◄ Experts look at footprints left in rock to find out about different types of dinosaur. This print was made by an anyklosaur.

► Thyreophora like this ankylosaur *Talarurus* may have had pads of cartilage at the bottom of their feet to protect them from wear and tear.

SORTED:

GIGANTSPINOSAURUS

DESPITE ITS NAME, *GIGANTSPINOSAURUS* WAS ACTUALLY ONLY A MEDIUM-SIZED STEGOSAUR. THIS "GIANT-SPINED LIZARD" GETS ITS NAME FROM ITS LARGE SHOULDER SPIKES.

QUICK FACTS

PERIOD:
Late Jurassic

LIVED IN:
China

LENGTH:
14 feet (4.2 m)

WEIGHT:
1,540 pounds (700 kg)

LONG LEGS

Like other stegosaurs, *Gigantspinosaurus* had long back legs compared to its front ones. The dinosaur was tallest at the hips, which were very wide. From there, the body sloped down to a low-slung head. Its front legs were thick and strong.

FEET AND TOES

Fossils of *Gigantspinosaurus*'s back feet have been found. These show that the back feet were a bit like an elephant's, with three blunt toes. The front feet had five toes, which gave better balance and grip on the ground.

SPIKES AND PLATES

Experts think that *Gigantspinosaurus* may have been one of the first stegosaurs. This is partly because of the huge, hooked spikes on its shoulders, which were a feature of early members of this group. *Gigantspinosaurus*'s plates were also quite small compared with those of later stegosaurs.

DINOMIGHTY!

The huge, hooked spines on the *Gigantspinosaurus*'s shoulders were as long as its front legs!

HEAD, MOUTH, AND TEETH

ALTHOUGH THE STEGOSAURS AND ANKYLOSAURS LOOKED DIFFERENT IN MANY WAYS, THEY ALL HAD SIMILAR SHAPED HEADS AND TYPES OF TEETH. MOST THYREOPHORA WERE HERBIVORES, WHICH MEANS THEY ATE ONLY PLANTS. SOME ANKYLOSAURS MAY HAVE ALSO EATEN INSECTS.

Thyreophora had low, flat skulls and snouts, shaped a bit like a spout. Stegosaur skulls were narrow, which meant there wasn't much room for big jaw muscles. The ankylosaurs had wider skulls, so they may have had stronger jaws.

▲ Some thyreophora had a horny beak that they used to bite the leaves off plants. This is the skull of the ankylosaur *Saichania*.

A stegosaur's bite was probably about as powerful as a dog's. With their big bodies, it seems surprising that they had such weak jaws. However, they didn't need strong jaws because they didn't chew their food properly. Instead, they tore at plant matter and swallowed it down.

Thyreophora mostly fed on plants such as mosses, ferns, conifers, and fruits. This diet was tough on the teeth!

Considering how much they ate, stegosaurs and ankylosaurs had quite small teeth. These were arranged in either straight or S-shaped rows in the mouth. The tops of the teeth were leaf-shaped, which was useful for shredding plants.

Like other herbivores, the stegosaurs may have had gastroliths. These small stones in the stomach would have helped to grind up plant matter to assist with digestion. However, experts don't know for sure.

The early stegosaur *Huayangosaurus* had teeth at the front of its mouth. Later species didn't have this feature.

SORTED:

PINACOSAURUS

QUICK FACTS

PERIOD:
Late Cretaceous

LIVED IN:
Asia

LENGTH:
16 feet (5 m)

WEIGHT:
up to 6,600 pounds (3,000 kg)

***PINACOSAURUS* WAS A MEDIUM-SIZED DINOSAUR WITH A SIMILAR BODY SHAPE AND ARMOR TO ITS ANKYLOSAUR RELATIVES. BUT *PINACOSAURUS* SKULLS SHOW SOME UNUSUAL FEATURES.**

HEAD

Pinacosaurus means "plank lizard." It was named after the flat bones that protected its head. However, its skull is unusual because the small plates covered only part of its head, not all of it like in other ankylosaurs. *Pinacosaurus* had a collar made out of bony plates, which protected its short neck.

NOSTRILS

This dinosaur also had unusual nostrils. Each one was a large hollow that contained several smaller holes. Experts aren't sure why they evolved like this. It may have been a way for *Pinacosaurus* to identify its own type when choosing a mate. Or the nostrils may have been part of a special system that helped them breathe in their dry environment.

DINOMIGHTY!

There were few predators in the time and place that *Pinacosaurus* lived. The vicious *Velociraptor* might have attacked, but *Pinacosaurus* could have defended itself with its huge tail club.

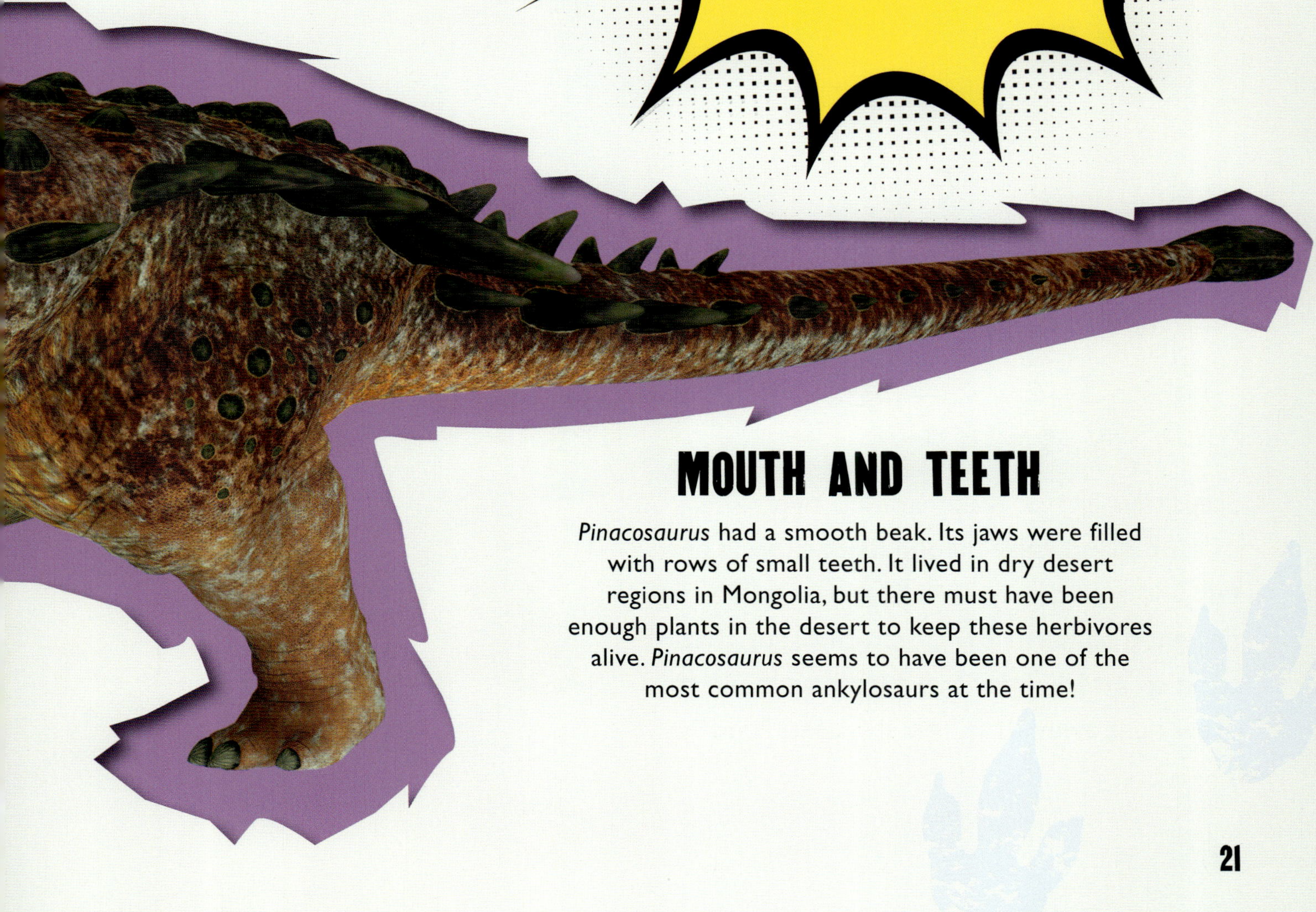

MOUTH AND TEETH

Pinacosaurus had a smooth beak. Its jaws were filled with rows of small teeth. It lived in dry desert regions in Mongolia, but there must have been enough plants in the desert to keep these herbivores alive. *Pinacosaurus* seems to have been one of the most common ankylosaurs at the time!

STEGOSAUR ARMOR

THE TWO GROUPS OF THYREOPHORA EACH HAD DIFFERENT TYPES OF ARMOR. AND THERE'S NO MISTAKING A STEGOSAUR! THIS IS THE ONLY GROUP OF DINOSAURS TO HAVE UPRIGHT BONY BACK PLATES.

Stegosaur armor was made up of a series of scutes and spikes along its backbone and tail. The spikes may have been defensive, designed to harm any other dinosaur that tried to attack. They may also have been to draw heat away from the stegosaur's body.

The plates grew out of the skin, not the skeleton. Some experts think that they may also have been covered in skin.

The plates were arranged in two rows down the back. In *Stegosaurus*, they were arranged in an alternating pattern. In most other stegosaurs, the plates were side by side. When stegosaur plates were first discovered, experts thought they lay flat against the body!

Stegosaurus and some other stegosaurs had huge spikes at the end of their tail. Some fossil spikes have been found that are damaged at the ends, and skeletons of big carnivores, such as *Allosaurus*, have been found with wounds like the holes made by these spikes. This suggests that stegosaurs used their tail for defending themselves.

The tail spikes of a stegosaur are arranged in a pattern called a thagomizer.

SORTED:

KENTROSAURUS

KENTROSAURUS ("SHARP-POINT LIZARD") WAS ONE OF THE SMALLEST STEGOSAURS—ONLY HALF THE SIZE OF A *STEGOSAURUS*! ITS SMALL SIZE MAY HAVE BEEN ONE REASON WHY *KENTROSAURUS* WAS SO WELL-ARMORED.

QUICK FACTS

PERIOD:
Late Jurassic

LIVED IN:
Africa

LENGTH:
15 feet (4.5 m)

WEIGHT:
4,410 pounds(2,000 kg)

BACK PLATES

Kentrosaurus had seven pairs of upright plates, from its head down its back. Experts once thought that the plates were just a form of protection, but now they think differently. The plates may have changed color as blood flowed into them, which could have been a way for *Kentrosaurus* to attract a mate. The plates may also have conducted heat away from the body.

DINOMIGHTY!

Many armored dinosaurs traveled alone, but *Kentrosaurus* may have been a herd animal. The remains of about 70 *Kentrosauruses* were found together in one site in Tanzania, Africa.

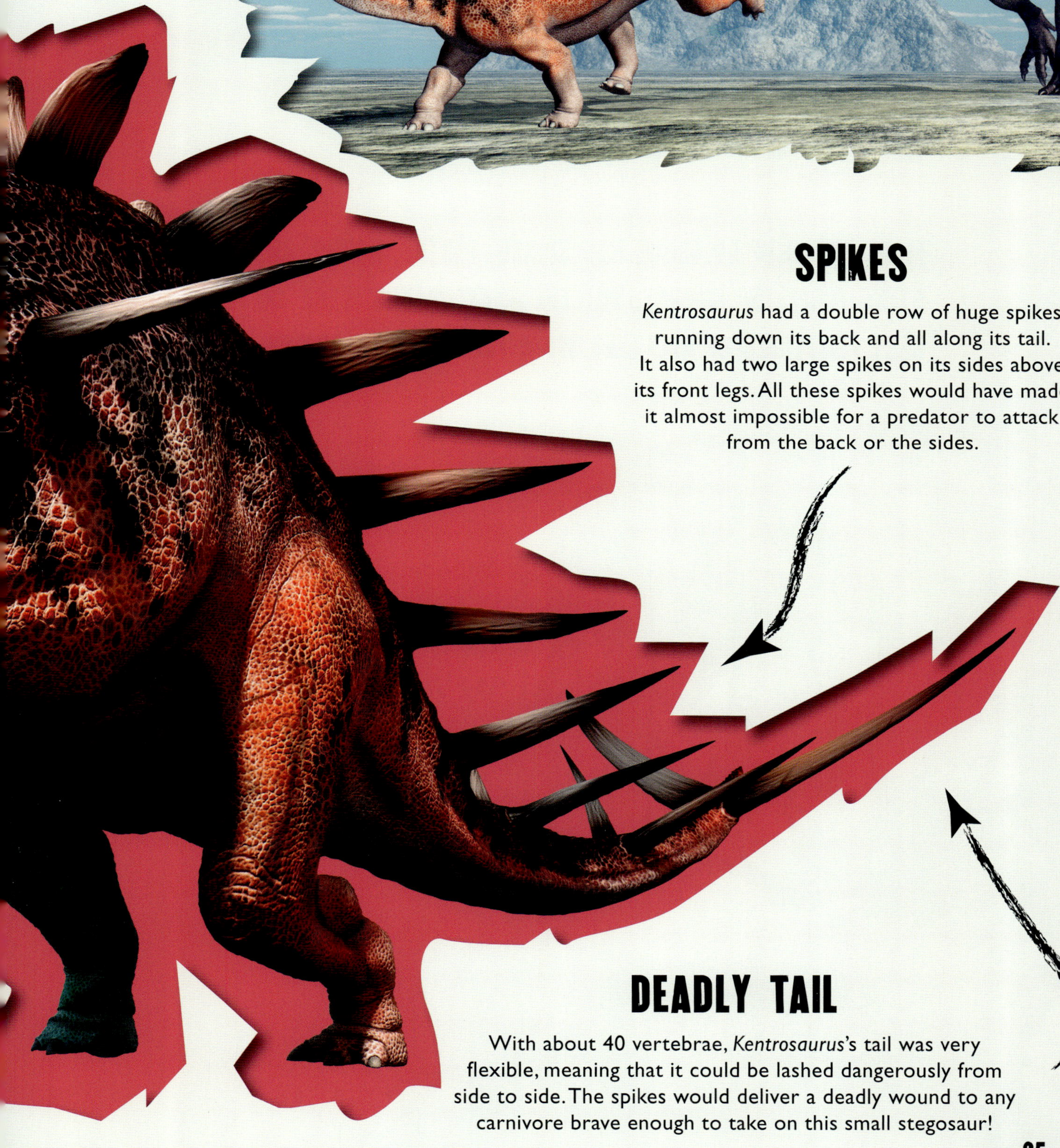

SPIKES

Kentrosaurus had a double row of huge spikes running down its back and all along its tail. It also had two large spikes on its sides above its front legs. All these spikes would have made it almost impossible for a predator to attack from the back or the sides.

DEADLY TAIL

With about 40 vertebrae, *Kentrosaurus*'s tail was very flexible, meaning that it could be lashed dangerously from side to side. The spikes would deliver a deadly wound to any carnivore brave enough to take on this small stegosaur!

ANKLYOSAUR ARMOR

MANY TYPES OF DINOSAUR HAD SPIKES, PLATES, HORNS, AND OTHER FORMS OF DEFENSE. BUT THE ANKYLOSAURS WERE THE BEST PROTECTED OF ALL. THEY WORE FULL SUITS OF ARMOR!

Ankylosaurs had scutes, or osteoderms, all over their bodies. These interlocking plates completely covered their back and flanks. They were embedded in the dinosaur's skin.

➤ Plates of bone even covered the ankylosaurs' heads.

On top of the scutes, many ankylosaurs also had a series of bony spikes. On some species, the spikes were made of thick, strong bone. They were probably defensive armor. On other ankylosaurs, the spikes were made of thin, brittle bone that would have broken easily under attack. These may have a had a different purpose–perhaps for display or to get rid of heat like a stegosaur's plates.

On *Talarurus*, the spikes ran from the head right down to the thick tail club.

Another feature of the ankylosaurs was their tail clubs. These were made from large pieces of bone fused together. Some experts think these were a weapon against other species. But others argue that if this was the case, baby ankylosaurs would have them–and they didn't. The tail clubs were more likely to be used for fighting members of their own species.

The tail club may have been used to cause serious damage to much larger dinosaurs.

SORTED:

EUOPLOCEPHALUS

OF ALL THE ANKYLOSAURS, BIG *EUOPLOCEPHALUS* WAS ONE OF THE BEST PROTECTED. PLATES, SPIKES, STUDS, AND A CLUBBED TAIL ALL COMBINED TO MAKE THIS DINOSAUR DIFFICULT TO ATTACK!

QUICK FACTS

PERIOD:
Late Cretaceous

LIVED IN:
North America

LENGTH:
23 feet (7 m)

WEIGHT:
4,410 pounds
(2,000 kg)

BONY HEAD

Euoplocephalus's head was protected by small plates made up of bones fused together like a jigsaw puzzle. It even had bones protecting its eyes, with bony "shutters" beneath the skin of its eyelids.

BACK ARMOR

Strips of thick, scaly skin ran all down *Euoplocephalus*'s back, from the neck to the tail. The tail itself was studded with bony spikes–long ones at the top of the back and shorter ones further down. *Euoplocephalus* also had spikes above its front legs and bony studs on its back ones.

TAIL

The tail club was huge. It was supported by strong, rod-like bones in the skeleton at the end of the tail. The base of the tail had lots of muscles, so it was very strong. But it was also flexible, so *Euoplocephalus* could swing it easily.

DINOMIGHTY!

A single blow from *Euoplocephalus*'s clubbed tail could break a *Tyrannosaurus rex*'s leg!

GLOSSARY

ADAPTED – changed to suit a particular environment better

ASTEROID – a large rock that forms in space and orbits the sun

CARNIVORE – an animal that eats meat

CARTILAGE – a strong but flexible tissue in the body

EVOLVE – to change and develop gradually over time

FLANKS – the sides of an animal between the ribs and the hips

FOSSIL – the shape of a plant or animal that has been preserved in rock for a very long time

HERBIVORE – an animal that eats only plants and fruit

MASS EXTINCTION – the death of many living things, when species stop existing completely

MATE – a reproductive partner

OSTEODERMS – lumps of bone in the skin of an animal

PALEONTOLOGIST – a scientist who studies dinosaurs and prehistoric life

PREDATOR – an animal that hunts and kills other animals for food

QUADRUPED – describing an animal that walks on four legs rather than two

SCUTES – the covering of bone or horn over the osteoderms on the back of an animal

SKULL – the bones that make up the head and face

SPECIES – a group of living things that are closely related and share similar features

SUB-GROUP – a group of animals within a larger category that have particular features in common

VERTEBRAE – the bones that make up the spine, or backbone (singular: vertebra)

FURTHER INFORMATION

BOOKS

Jackson, Tom. *T. Rex vs. Ankylosaurus: Prehistoric Showdown*. Minneapolis, MN: Lerner Publications, 2026.

Taylor, Paul D. *Fossil*. New York, NY: DK Publishing, 2023.

ACTIVITY

Use the information in this book to design a new stegosaur or ankylosaur. Remember to include the features of whichever thyreophora type you choose. Then give your dinosaur a name.

WEBSITES

www.nhm.ac.uk/discover/dinosaurs.html
Find out all about the dinosaurs at the website of the Natural History Museum found in the UK.

https://kids.nationalgeographic.com/animals/prehistoric
Explore more about dinosaurs here.

INDEX